the fullness OF FAITHFULNESS

To order additional copies of *The Fullness of Faithfulness,*
compiled by Lori Bryan, editor, **call 1-800-765-6955.**

Visit us at **www.reviewandherald.com** for information on
other Review and Herald® products.

The *fullness* OF FAITHFULNESS

LORI BRYAN, EDITOR

REVIEW AND HERALD® PUBLISHING ASSOCIATION

Since 1861 | www.reviewandherald.com

Published by Review and Herald® Publishing Association, Hagerstown, MD 21741-1119

This book was
Edited by Vesna Mirkovich
Copyedited by Megan Mason
Cover design by Et Tu Design
Interior designed by Emily Ford / Review and Herald® Design Center
Typeset: Minion Pro 13/15

PRINTED IN U.S.A.

17 16 15 14 13   5 4 3 2 1

Library of Congress Cataloging-in-Publication Data

The fullness of faithfulness/Lori Bryan, ed.
    pages cm
1. Christian women—Religious life—Anecdotes. 2. Christian stewardship—Anecdotes. I. Bryan, Lori, 1963-   .
    BV4527.F86 2014
    248.8'43—dc23
                    2012049328

ISBN 978-0-8280-2717-5

I will sing of the Lord's great love forever;
with my mouth I will make your faithfulness
known through all generations.

—Psalm 89:1, NIV

Contents

Foreword 9

Family

My Heart's Desire, by Stephanie Peterson McMillan 13

Strength From Above, by Dawn Ebanks 17

Let the Lord Lead, by Margaret E. Humphrey Richardson 20

Where Is Thy Flock? by Vinette Brown Dye. 24

Faith

My Red Sea Experience, by Louise Davis 31

Got Faith? by Wanda Jenkins 35

Can He Touch Me? by R. Chris Bearce 38

The Hug From God, by Charlotte Ishkanian 41

Fellowship

Sisters, by Linda R. Anderson. 47

Drawn by Love, by Judy B. Dent 51

A Hot Meal and a Smile, by Kristina Smith 55

Of Neighbors and Friends, by Carol Barron. 58

Finance

Trusting His Promises, by Julie Bryan 65

I Do, by Melissa Reid 68

He Never Fails, by Marialyce Fordham 72

I Am That Steward, by Kathleen Murrell 76

Fitness

Get Up, Girl! by Gina Brown 83

Living Bodies, Living Foods:
The Choice Is Yours, by Grazyna Dabrowska 86

The Stewardship of the Mind, by Victoria Joiner Miller 89

My Healer and Friend, by April Hardinge 93

Foreword

What is your concept of stewardship? Is it something you even think about? Perhaps you don't have a clear understanding of what stewardship really is. Unfortunately, many people associate stewardship with poorly prepared or boring sermons on tithing. You've heard them. During the sermon your mind starts to wander, and you're tempted to surf the Internet or play games on your mobile device.

Mistakenly, stewardship has been narrowly defined in terms of financial faithfulness, but its scope is much broader than merely returning tithe and giving an offering. Stewardship to the Christian is management of *all* that God has entrusted to us. We partner with Him to bring returns on His investments. All that we have and all that we are belong to our Creator. We have the privilege to use what He has given us to help grow His kingdom.

This book presents stewardship from a different perspective, one that reflects the stewardship of women. Some of God's most faithful stewards are women. Despite the fact that many women juggle family, work, church, and other duties, they are committed to practicing stewardship in their everyday lives. Through it all, they are learning to trust God for everything as they grow in grace.

The following pages contain testimonies from 20 women who in their times of hardship as well as happiness, in sickness and in health, have experienced God's unfailing love for them. Their stories cover five areas of stewardship—family, faith, fellowship, finance, and fitness. Your strength will be renewed as you read each heartfelt testimony, and you will see how God lovingly cares for His people. I invite you to enter their world and experience the joy of stewardship.

—LORI BRYAN, EDITOR

Family

My Heart's Desire

Before you were formed in the womb I knew you;
before you were born I selected you.
—Jeremiah 1:5, Clear Word

When my husband and I were dating, it was an ongoing joke as to how many children we would have; he wanted more, and I wanted less. A little more than a year after we were married, we began trying to conceive and were given devastating news—I would most likely never be able to become pregnant. Since my husband is a physician, we tried everything medical science could offer to give us the family we desired. But after 10 years of trying, we finally abandoned our resolve and accepted the reality that we would remain childless.

We proceeded to build a beautiful country home and made modifications to potentially accommodate our parents, should the need arise, and some extra storage areas. In the midst of building, we got a call from a doctor we had last seen seven years prior. Someone had called their office looking for an African-American couple to adopt a child. They contacted us! The extra downstairs room would become a nursery!

We were present for our daughter's birth. What joy—for me to become a mother and for my husband, an OB/GYN, to finally hold his own child! God had seen fit to bless us with a family after all.

This being our first child, we didn't know what "normal" things to look for, but we knew that Olivia was a handful. By the time she was 3 years old I noticed that she didn't quite "fit in" with the other children at social gatherings, and so I wanted to have her tested. My husband refused. I then enrolled her in a day care to help alleviate the challenges I was facing and thought, *They deal with children all day, every day; if something is not right, certainly they will notice.*

One morning as I was preparing to take Olivia to day care, out of the blue God spoke to my heart. He said, "I chose you to be her mother."

One morning as I was preparing to take Olivia to day care, out of the blue God spoke to my heart. He said, "I chose you to be her mother." I very flippantly replied, "I know. I know the whole adoption story." He in turn said, "No! I chose *you* to be her mother." That evening, when I picked Olivia up, the day-care director said she had concerns and needed to speak with us the next morning. I don't know why, but autism is all that came to my mind at the time, even though Olivia didn't seem to display the telltale signs of autism I was aware of. She was a happy-go-lucky kid.

That night our world changed. My husband and I both cried and cried. And cried some more for a solid month. It didn't seem fair that this should happen to us. We had waited so long and had tried so hard to have a family, and now this—a child with a special need. No!

As grieved as we were, we still proceeded with all the testing we could. After one month Olivia was placed in a special-needs preschool with an excellent teacher who loved working with children with autism. All of the testing diagnosed Olivia with classic autism. Before the year was out, we started an intensive in-home therapy. That extra storage room modification was the perfect spot for the isolated 40 hours of therapy per week that she needed.

As time progressed and Olivia approached school age, it was again God's leading that directed us to homeschool Olivia. Homeschooling allows me the flexibility to tailor the curriculum to her abilities or needs as they arise. Currently, at the time this story is being written, she is completing the third grade. She's a smart, bright, and intelligent girl whose brain is wired just a little differently. My mother always assures me of the blessing I am to Olivia.

Just as I ask Olivia to trust me completely because I am her mother and know what is best for her, I have to realize God feels the exact same way about me.

God saw fit to bring Olivia to our family so that she could be prepared for the kingdom! I have no doubt that He also brought her to us so we could more closely rely on Him for strength to endure the task He has set before us. We constantly pray for patience, wisdom, and understanding. Above all, when these things are not granted, we pray for faith. From before the time Olivia was even conceived, God had a plan for her life.

Parenting has been such an eye-opener for me, especially in deepening my understanding of God's love for not only me but for all living, breathing beings on this earth. When I reprimand Olivia, "How many times do I have to tell you before you understand . . . ?" I can hear God asking me the same thing. How many times will I repeat the same mistakes before I acknowledge that I have to completely surrender to the will of my Father? Just as I ask Olivia to trust me completely because I am her mother and know what is best for her, I have to realize God feels the exact same way about me.

We are being stewards of the trust God gave to us in giving us Olivia. Together, as a family, we await Christ's appearing.

Stephanie Peterson McMillan is a wife of 24 years and stay-at-home mom to one. She enjoys photography, genealogy, scrapbooking, crocheting, traveling, and time spent with family and friends. Above all, she longs for all her family to see the Savior face to face.

Strength From Above

But they that wait upon the Lord shall renew their strength;
they shall mount up with wings as eagles;
they shall run, and not be weary;
and they shall walk, and not faint.
—Isaiah 40:31

Dawn, this is your neighbor Barbara, from down the street. I'm here at the hospital with your mother. She has something to tell you." There was some rustling, and then my mother's voice came through in a tone I had never heard. "Dawn, dear, your father is gone. He's gone."

With these words, the biggest adjustment of my life began. My mother never asked me to come, but being a physical therapist and having worked for so many years with those who were elderly, I knew that my mother was not going to be able to manage the house on her own. Knowing that I could adjust more easily than she could at 79, I sold my home and, within five months of that fateful call, moved to Palm Bay, Florida.

"Dawn, dear, your father is gone. He's gone."

I wish I could say that the transition was an easy one. I missed my job, my church, my friends, and the many cultural attractions I liked to frequent in my spare time. I wondered if perhaps I had made a mistake in making so drastic a move.

At first I was more of a roommate, handling the duties of the house that required the most brawn. Several months after I arrived, however, Mom began to have pain in her right shoulder from a worn-out shoulder replacement. Mom had surgery in Tampa to correct the problem. I spent the nights with her in the hospital, grateful that I was near enough to help by making the many five-hour round-trip visits for the surgery and her follow-up care.

The dear mother who had cared for me so tenderly for so many years was now fully in my charge and increasingly in need of the same tender care.

It seems Mom had no sooner recovered from her surgery than the hurricanes of 2004 hit us—hard. Our roof failed, and we were forced to hurriedly move from our home until it was repaired. We remained in a rental home for 10 months, as two thirds of our home was stripped down to the studs and rebuilt. Despite the harrowing circumstances, and often feeling overwhelmed, I was glad that I was there to assist Mom in a situation that I could not have handled effectively from far away.

As the years passed we faced other medical crises that gradually began to change the dynamic of our relationship. Mom had to have yet another shoulder surgery and the pinning of a broken hip. She now had to depend on a walker for her mobility and was unable to perform many of her regular household tasks.

She developed seizures that took six years (and a trip to the well-known Mayo Clinic) to diagnose. The uncontrolled seizures caused her to have some short-term memory loss. The dear mother who had cared for me so tenderly for so many years was now fully in my charge and increasingly in need of the same tender care.

Although Mom's life circumstances changed dramatically over the years, her reaction to the changes was remarkable. Through it all she never complained, doubted, or gave in to despair. She was cheerful, singing songs of praise and speaking words of hope. Her favorite phrase was "the best is yet to be." She frequently expressed gratitude for the blessings in her life. She was always ready to speak of her God when given the opportunity. Despite her increasing life challenges, her relationship with God seemed to deepen. She still seemed, in spite of it all, filled with joy. I, on the other hand, had to pray often for God to give me the strength to deal with the ever-changing situation with the grace, love, and kindness that had been shown to me.

Long gone are the days I would pine for my "old life." I have made new friends, have found new places of interest, and am involved in church work. The time spent with Mom has been priceless and worth all the adjustments. I have had to rely on God more than ever before to help me cope with the increasing responsibility. He has been so faithful in providing just the help I need.

While God was busy taking care of the many requests I sent His way, He also managed, in a way that only He could, to do a little work on me, too. I learned to be grateful for the simple things in life. I learned that happiness is a choice, and I have begun to make it my choice every day. I have become more patient. I now know that with God there can be joy in all circumstances. I know that God hears prayers and He will provide. Having seen God repeatedly come through right on time, I can say that my faith now stands solid.

The road has not always been an easy one, but I am sure it was the one God intended for me. In choosing to be a blessing to my greatest treasure, my mother, God has truly blessed me, too.

Dawn Ebanks writes from Palm Bay, Florida, where she enjoys entertaining, gardening, and visiting museums.

Let the Lord Lead

For your Father knoweth what things
ye have need of, before ye ask him.
—Matthew 6:8

Growing up in a ministerial family as a PK, or preacher's kid, I have always been exposed to the notion of what a Christian family should be. Whether through my own experiences or from listening to the writings of Ellen G. White as read by my parents around the breakfast table most mornings, I developed my own sense of what my home would be like one day. I was never comfortable seeing my four older brothers occasionally "rumble" or wrestle about on the floor, or hear discord in their voices as all my siblings got on one another's nerves on long trips! I determined in my heart that my children would love one another and "be kindly affectioned one to another with brotherly love" (Rom. 12:10, KJV). I also knew that children were an inheritance from the Lord and that they should also be taught to love Him with all their hearts. I knew that as I followed the Lord's lead, this would one day become my reality.

God blessed me with a wonderful husband who, like my father, is a minister. We shared the same values in Christian living and even read through Ellen G. White's *The Adventist Home before* we got married, to form a pact on how our home would eventually be! However, knowing that a ministerial family is much like that of a medical doctor's family in that pastors, like doctors, are often absent from the home for large periods of time, I knew that the brunt of the parenting would fall on me. My husband would rarely even be able to sit with us in church.

In my commitment to God, I resolved that I never, ever wanted Him to question me on the whereabouts of the "flock" He had given me.

God blessed us with three children, who indeed had to be taught every step of the way how to be Christlike in manner and behavior. I had to teach them not only how to share but how to truly love one another. When one got hurt, I would use the incident as an opportunity to teach them lessons in empathy and sympathy. We always disciplined in love. We had thorough discussions on wrongdoing, implemented consequences as needed, and applied disciplinary measures that varied as widely as the children's personalities. Lessons were learned, and characters were developed.

While in church, I rarely used the mother's room, because I wanted my children to experience the sanctuary as a place of reverence as well as love. While in the sanctuary, I was led to purposefully "love on" my children where they could hear the organ, singing, praying, and preaching going on around them. I cuddled them, held them closely during the service, gave them full eye contact and care, and thus instilled in them a strong love for God, so much so that they love church now as grown people. I attribute my intentional experience with my children to the Holy Spirit speaking to my heart when another adult PK once gave a testimony of how he hated church because that's where he got the most spankings. Sadly, he never wanted to set foot in a church again once he became an adult. In my commitment to God I resolved that I never ever wanted Him to question me on the whereabouts of "the flock" He had given me.

Time, energy, and a commitment to Christian education for our children led me to homeschool them during their earliest years. My focus was that parents ought to be their child's first teachers. It certainly fostered in our children the feeling of security and confidence in their learning experience rather than feelings of separation anxiety. They were taught of the Lord throughout their educational curriculum. At an early age they experienced a meaningful relationship with God; they worshipped Him with us and were delighted to witness God listening and answering their prayers! God remains real in their lives, even now that they are in their 20s.

A church member, disturbed by the fact that my boys were back in town and not away at school, told her husband of her strong impression to help financially.

Christian education is a costly endeavor that has eternal benefits. We have faced financial hardships, especially as college tuition arose simultaneously for three children, but God has always attended to our needs. Just this past fall we couldn't see financially how we were going to be able to send our twin sons back to Oakwood University, where they had finished their freshman year. We drove down to Huntsville, Alabama, as a family unit, hoping upon hope that the twins and their older sister, who was finishing up her education, could all reenroll. However, the twins did not receive any financial aid, so we brought them back home, thinking that they would take a year off to work.

When we returned to church the following Sabbath and met with members who knew the boys were to have left for school, I knew the boys felt sheepish answering the questions of the members. I sat in my pew and prayed a brief prayer to God that He would provide a miracle similar to one given in a testimony by a single parent widower who was financially at his rope's end in sending his daughter to the same school and in whose circumstances God had intervened. Unbeknown to me, within 10 minutes God was answering my prayer! A church member, disturbed by the fact that my boys were back in town and *not* away at school, told her husband of her strong impression to help financially. He literally told my husband, before the sermon started, to pack our boys back up and drive them back to Alabama; they were going to help! I didn't find out what had transpired until I got in the car after church and my husband informed me. I shouted praise to God and cried tears of joy. My God had heard and answered my prayer in the shortest amount of time with the largest answer possible! He was happy with our stewardship and investment in educating our children, and He was swift in making it continue! Praise God, from whom all blessings flow!

Margaret E. Humphrey Richardson writes from Bowie, Maryland. She is an artist who enjoys teaching, singing, sewing, horseback riding, and arts and crafts.

Where is Thy Flock?

Lo, children are an heritage of the Lord:
and the fruit of the womb is his reward.
—Psalm 127:3

While collecting dirty dishes at a friend's potluck, I noticed a young couple with a newborn. I commented on how lovely it was to see a sleeping baby. The parents were flattered, and smiled. Still holding an armful of dishes, I fondly remarked at these being some of the best years of their lives! By the separate but synchronized look they each gave me, I detected they doubted that, as they exasperatedly asked me how long these "best years" would last.

Probing a little deeper, I asked what their plans were for raising their baby boy. That's when the young woman's countenance completely fell. She looked at me with the saddest, most despairing eyes. Drawing closer to me, she whispered, "I don't know." I asked if she was planning to stay at home with the baby. Almost helplessly she looked up at me and said, "I have to go back to work. I've been on bed rest for my whole pregnancy, and we need the money." By then *I* felt like crying! The concern on my face was hard to hide. I drew yet a little closer to her, so as to make the conversation a bit more private. Her husband had now stopped listening and had joined another of several conversations simultaneously going on in the room. Now, in a more hushed tone, this young woman—full of joy, yet full of confusion, and *so full of milk*—shared with me that she wanted to stay at home to nurse and raise her baby but that she just *couldn't* for financial reasons. They had just purchased their first home and were at capacity in debt. With every word she spoke I felt increasingly desperate to help her with this dilemma. *Lord,* I thought, *how do I help this woman see that this is Your baby whom You have entrusted to her?* Still holding the dishes, I crouched down close to where she sat, and began probing further. I asked her if they had bought the house on a joint salary or if they had qualified for the home on her husband's salary alone. Although her husband had qualified for the house on his salary alone, they really needed two incomes to "make ends meet," she explained.

My heart ached for this poor young mother. How could I help her see it is God's will for *every* baby to be taught of the Lord, especially from birth? I could see the tears welling up in her eyes. Here she was with an infant only days separated from her own flesh, and already she was talking of *work* and looking for someone to care for her brand-new, fresh-out-of–the-womb baby! After ending the conversation in intercessory prayer, I helped her collect herself as I collected my dishes and took them to the sink.

One thing was abundantly clear to me. The Bible says we are not our own (1 Cor. 6:19). Children are a trust from the Lord—*a heritage,* says the Word of God (Ps. 127:3). Given that they are not our own, do we have the right to decide what to do with them? Is it our privilege to make decisions for their welfare without so much as consulting with the true owner? No! We are bought with a price!

Who were Mary, Elizabeth, Hannah, and Jochebed? What kind of mothers were they? These are mothers who all knew they had been honored and had found favor with God. What these women also knew is that their babies were *not* their own—that they had been given the opportunity only to *steward* them, for God's glory.

What these women also knew is that their babies were not their own—that they had been given the opportunity only to steward them, for God's glory.

I once knew a man with a personality of a renegade. He used to say of his mother, "I came *through* her; I don't belong *to* her." It always made me laugh to hear him say that. But that sentiment is exactly what all these biblical mothers knew. They knew these special babies had come *through* them but never belonged *to* them. That realization changed the manner in which those babies were raised. Jochebed knew she couldn't do with that baby as she desired, even though she had given birth to him. For these women, that knowledge defined what those babies could watch, where they could go, what they could listen to, who their friends would be, or what they could eat or drink, for whatsoever they did, all had to be done to the glory of God (see 1 Cor. 10:31).

Friend of mine, are we any less than Jochebed, Mary, Elizabeth, or Hannah in God's eyes? Do not all children belong to God? Are not all Christian mothers employed by God just as Jochebed was employed by royalty to nurture, care for, and raise these babies to know who their true Father is? In a way, we are wet nurses, caring for babies who belong to a King! What an honor! What an awesome task! When we grasp these truths, when we realize that God blessed us with alimony for the care, keeping, and nurture of these babies, we will be ever mindful that one day we will have to stand before God in the judgment and answer the question "Where is the flock that was given thee, thy beautiful flock?"

Vinette Brown Dye is a freelance writer and professional educator. She is married to Rodney Dye and lives in Rock Hill, South Carolina, where she educates the couple's two sets of twins, Matthew and Madison, 11, and Joshua and Joseph, 13, at home. In her spare time she enjoys visits to the beach, providing hospitality to friends and strangers, and taking road trips with her family.

Faith

My Red Sea Experience

But he was pierced for our transgressions,
he was crushed for our iniquities;
the punishment that brought us peace was on him,
and by his wounds we are healed.
—Isaiah 53:5, NIV

From my childhood years my parents impressed upon me the importance of stewardship. Tithing was a regular practice in our house. As I grew older, I realized that stewardship involved more than just returning tithe. This realization hit home when I became more concerned about my personal ministry for the Lord. How could I witness for Him? I didn't think I had anything to say that was worth listening to. At the same time, I was asked to be part of a praise team at church. Though I felt I wasn't ready to lead the service in praise and worship, I said yes anyway. My faith in God would be severely tested; I had no idea how much.

Shortly after accepting the praise team position, I found a lump in my breast. After several examinations I was diagnosed with breast cancer. What a shock! No one in my family had ever had that disease. How could I praise God with a diagnosis like that? But here's how the Lord works when we trust Him.

One day a family friend who had fought and won her battle with cancer called me and gave me the scripture listed at the top of this testimony, Isaiah 53:5. She told me that I wasn't *going* to be healed; I was *already* healed! I just had to walk through the Red Sea.

Cancer was something I could not control. It was out of my hands. I knew the only way I could get through this was to trust God completely, regardless of the outcome. I wanted to be healed, but I had to surrender completely to His will. To me, this meant trusting God to lead me to the right people for treatment. Not having gone down this road before, I didn't know what to expect, and I cried constantly.

> *Cancer was something I could not control. It was out of my hands. I knew the only way I could get through this was to trust God completely, regardless of the outcome.*

When I went to consult with the surgeon, the first thing I saw upon entering his office was a picture of Jesus in the operating room standing behind a surgeon, guiding his hand! During my visit the surgeon shared that he was a cancer survivor and had undergone treatment. My tears continued, but now they were tears of release and deliverance.

I remember one Sabbath we sang Gary Mayes' "All Ye Faithful." When we got to the last verse, "Oh, I cannot live without, without Him. I cannot live without, without. Oh, I cannot live without, without Him, His name is Christ," I felt as if my heart would break; I couldn't even sing. I stood there with tears streaming down my face. When we left the sanctuary, one of my praise team members turned to me and said, "God will work this out for you, so go ahead and cry." I turned to her and said, "Oh, I'm not crying because I'm sad. I'm crying because I'm thankful that no matter what happens, I know God has this situation taken care of."

After seeing the surgeon, I consulted with the oncologist. I was pleased to find him very personable. His attitude regarding my treatment was positive. Surprisingly, I didn't find out until several years later that his practice was the top-ranking oncology practice in the country. Again, I felt God's grace and mercy. My trust in God to guide me to the right doctors enabled me to receive the best treatment available. Even my radiologist and his staff were friendly and professional, but it was more than that; God had led me to them.

The Lord used my children, too. My eldest never let me go to any treatment by myself. My oldest twin daughter was with me during the diagnosis and would repeat back to me what the doctor said because it was just too much for me to deal with at the time.

Even though I didn't always feel like it, I continued to serve on the praise team. There were Sabbaths that I had only enough energy to do just that. When I was done, I would get into the back of my daughter's car with my pillow and blanket and sleep while she drove us home.

Another Sabbath I could barely feel my feet because the chemotherapy was damaging the nerves in them. It wasn't until after the service that my goddaughter, a mere 4 years old, looked at my feet and told me I had my shoes on the wrong feet. I couldn't even feel them!

As I reflect on my Red Sea experience, I know that God led me to all the individuals who treated my disease and encouraged me. While participating with the praise team and choir, I learned a valuable stewardship lesson. I had asked God for a way to be a witness for Him. I believe He answered by giving me a story to tell. He allowed me to endure breast cancer and then be healed so that I can encourage others who are going through their own Red Sea experience. I'm a steward of the testimony He has given

He allowed me to endure breast cancer and then be healed so that I can encourage others who are going through their own Red Sea experience. I am a steward of the testimony He has given me to share.

me to share. Five years later it is still an overwhelming experience, but one that caused my faith to grow. Praise God!

Louise Davis is a compliance specialist at the University of Maryland and the proud mother of four grown daughters, Cherie, Dawn, Donna, and Elizabeth. She enjoys family time at home and fishing!

Got Faith?

Blessed be the Lord God, the God of Israel,
who only doeth wondrous things.
—Psalm 72:18

Today I asked my mother at what age I started walking. Her answer really didn't matter. I now know I didn't begin walking until I was 50 years old! "Fifty?" you ask. Let me explain.

Just days before my fiftieth birthday, I learned that the owners of the condo we were renting had decided to sell their condo. No problem! Although my husband's health didn't permit him to work, I had a good job, so we started looking for another place.

Weeks later, while reviewing my supervisor's e-mails (one of my duties as an executive assistant), I accidentally opened an e-mail that clearly was not intended for me to read. They were scheduling a meeting to discuss my termination! My heart sank. Everything after that was a blur, but somehow I was able to drive myself home. No, I didn't have a home. I was renting, and they were selling. How on earth were we going to find a new home, knowing that I was about to be laid off? So many questions, and not one answer in sight! I felt totally abandoned by my employer, but even more by God. Where were we to go? What were we to do?

For the next few weeks I spent my days at work pretending I had never read that dreaded e-mail, and my nights packing, cleaning, and crying. How do you look for a new place, knowing your job is ending? How do you look for a job, not knowing where you're going to live? *For we walk by faith, not by sight!* I couldn't see the light at the end of the tunnel. All I saw was darkness, and all I felt was abandoned.

How do you look for a new place, knowing your job is ending? How do you look for a job, not knowing where you're going to live?

After finally being told I was going to be laid off (just a week before we were to move out), we figured this would be a good time to take an extended "vacation" and visit my sister in Florida. She had just been offered a new job, in Ohio, and was packing up her house. *Really, God? Are You kidding me?* I found myself sitting on a plane, totally exhausted after spending our last night in the condo cleaning and making one final trip to the storage unit filled with all our possessions. *Is this what it's come to, Lord? Have You totally abandoned me? Is my whole life summed up in this 10' x 10' unit?*

After we returned to Maryland, some wonderful friends opened their home up to us. We spent days petitioning the Lord. We laughed, prayed, and shared God's blessings, but after a few weeks we had to make a decision. They weren't putting us out; we just wanted to get on with our lives. We had made friends in Florida, there were business opportunities there, and the weather was gorgeous, so we decided to make that move. We had researched housing while we were there, so we figured we had enough money to last us a month or two until we found something. And then it hit us! We were actually leaving our friends, our church family, our home for the past 25 years! *For we walk by faith, not by sight!*

Starting over was not easy. How do you fill out a rental application with no job? After going to several places without any success, we decided to stay with my godfather in another city until something came through, which meant searching for housing online. After inquiring about several properties, we made appointments all on the same day and drove down to look at them. Frustrated because neither of the houses were what we expected, we prayed and completely turned it over to the Lord. We had stepped out in faith, doing all we could do. Now it was time to trust God. As we were driving away, something told me to stop. *For we walk by faith, not by sight!* We were in the same neighborhood where we had stayed with my sister. It was familiar. It was safe. As we drove through one last time, I was impressed to look, and I saw a "For Rent" sign we had never seen before, even though we had driven through this development numerous times. God was working things out. We called the owner, explained our situation, and left it in God's hands.

We have now lived here for the past year and a half. Our move to Florida has been one of adventure as we have seen the hand of God direct our paths and work on our behalf. Our walk of faith has not been an easy one, but it has truly sustained us as we trust in God's divine guidance. We continue to seek God's will for our lives here, but the blessings He's already given us are a clear indication that God has a purpose or a use for everything that happens, and as we continue to trust in His will, we will continue to walk in faith, knowing that everything is going to be all right.

We had stepped out in faith, doing all we could do. Now it was time to trust God.

Wanda Jenkins writes from Jacksonville, Florida, and enjoys writing résumés and providing creative solutions and idea development for small businesses.

Can He Touch Me?

For I, the Lord your God,
will hold your right hand, saying to you,
"Fear not, I will help you."
—Isaiah 41:13, NKJV

As I lay in bed staring up at the ceiling with tears trickling into my ears, I began to replay the confrontation within me. *Why, God? Why? I can't change how I feel. I can't stop the pain. I have no hope, and that scares me.* The breakup of a marriage and a family is literally a crying shame.

Although I very much appreciated how my friends and family tried to help me with the feelings of betrayal, abandonment, fear, and the loss of self-worth, there were times that I just wanted to run away from it all. Nighttime gave me that escape. After work, after the evening with my two precious boys, after the bedtime games and rituals, I would retreat to my room and to the darkness that surrounded me. Not wanting my young boys, Jay and Paul, to know the extent of my grief, I did my

One thing about lying in bed and staring at the ceiling—it forced me to look up.

38

best to "put on a good face." I even learned how to cry without making a sound.

My room also became the place where the seemingly endless questioning went on and on as my mind cycled through the what fors, the how comes, the what ifs, and the unfairness of it all. *When will the pain stop? Will this emptiness ever go away? Will I ever be loved again? Who will ever want someone like me?* My silent cries seemed doomed to be unanswered.

One thing about lying in bed and staring at the ceiling—it forced me to look up. As a marginal, nondenominational "Christian," I believed in God, but I believed Him to be someone or something beyond the ceiling. I didn't really understand who He was or what He expected from me, or vice versa. Prayer was reserved for life-or-death crises; otherwise, I didn't see the need to bother Him. But who was this personal and loving God some of my friends were telling me about? If He was such a loving God, why was He letting this happen to me and my boys? Would He, could He, help me?

Now, as a Seventh-day Adventist, I have learned without a doubt that our awesome, loving God is personally involved in His children's lives and that nothing is beyond His reach.

One night after the boys had finally dropped off to sleep, I was feeling especially desperate as I went to my room. "Why, God? Why? I can't change how I feel. I can't stop the pain. I have no hope. I know You exist, but at the same time, I don't know how You can help me. I hate the loneliness, and I miss how it was when my husband would put his arms around me to comfort me. I know this sounds stupid, but I need a cuddle. But You are so far away, too far away. And how can You give me what I need when You aren't touchable? It's not as if You have arms that could reach through the ceiling and hold me.

And if You did somehow make that happen, I would be scared to death. Maybe You can't help me with this."

Suddenly the bedroom door burst open, and the light from the hallway filled the corner of the room. Startled, I defensively pulled the covers to my chin. On came the overhead light as my young boys burst into the room, dragging two big packing boxes. I lay there speechless as they frantically ripped open the flaps of the boxes and began to throw stuffed animals on my bed. In quick order they lifted the first box, then the other, and poured the last of the contents onto the already-big pile of furry toys. Then Jay and Paul dove into the mass of critters as if it were a pile of autumn leaves.

"What in the world is going on with you two?" I sat up and asked them in amazement.

"We thought you could use a cuddle, Mom. So we got you all our cuddle toys from the storage room!" Then, with one on my left and one on my right, the boys each put an arm around my shoulder and said, "I love you, Mom!"

That was more than 20 years ago, but the story is so vivid to me—even today as I tell it again. Now, as a Seventh-day Adventist, I have learned without a doubt that our awesome, loving God is personally involved in His children's lives and that nothing is beyond His reach. After that night there have been many times that I have trusted Him to lead me through other valleys, and He has been faithful! Every day I praise His name and ask Him to use me to touch others for Jesus.

How truly blessed I am—from out of the darkness to the Light of the world—"O the joy that floods my soul!"

R. Chris Bearce writes from Berrien Springs, Michigan, and enjoys working for the Lord.

The Hug From God

*Call to me and I will answer you
and tell you great and unsearchable things you do not know.*
—Jeremiah 33:3, NIV

It was a sultry summer day. My two preschool sons were tired of playing outside, and it was too hot to stay in the un–air-conditioned house for long. Their cranky whining awoke my infant daughter from her nap.

I was a stay-at-home mom, but I worked several different part-time jobs to supplement my husband's sporadic income. I had just finished sorting the monthly bills, trying to decide which ones to pay with the little money we had. I had cut every corner possible—sometimes several times—in order to pay the bills and avoid debt. But there was always some urgent need—an unexpected medical bill, new tires for the aging car, an unscheduled fuel bill. With joy and fervent prayers, we always first gave God His tithe and our offerings, claiming the promise that He would honor our commitment to Him.

Going back to work full-time wasn't an option with three small children at home. I wasn't willing to let a babysitter raise my precious children so I could work full-time.

I wish . . . I wish . . . I wasn't even sure what I wished for. Maybe I just needed a hug from someone I loved who didn't have jelly on his hands.

With a lump in my throat that threatened to choke into a sob, I walked out into the sultry backyard and filled the boys' little plastic wading pool with fresh water. Maybe hearing their laughter would make me feel better.

Strange, I thought. The boys run through here several times a day. How did they not destroy this bush?

I wandered across the shady yard toward the garden, when I noticed something unusual. Standing in the middle of the well-worn path that led to the garden plot stood a small bush. *Strange,* I thought. *The boys run through here several times a day. How did they not destroy this bush?* I stooped and looked at the plant. A gasp squeezed from my throat. It was a raspberry bush, a perfectly formed raspberry bush.

I knelt beside the bush and touched a leaf. It hadn't rained in several days, yet there wasn't any dust on the leaves. A sense of awe flowed over me like a cool breeze. Three raspberries, fully ripe and ready to pick, hung from the fragile branches.

Raspberries, my favorite fruit, and far too expensive to even *think* about buying. "How . . . ?" Words would come, but tears came instead as I realized the answer to my unspoken question. "God, it was You, wasn't it?" I managed to whisper. "You want me to know You're here, You care."

They're yours, a thought brushed through my mind. *Enjoy them.* I reached down and picked the first raspberry, sun-warmed and soft. Slowly I touched it to my tongue, closed my eyes, and savored the delicate flavor of a fruit I hadn't dared even think about buying. *I will never leave you or forsake you*, the promise whispered as I tasted the second berry. *I am with you always.* God's familiar words took on new, personal, and delicious meaning as I tasted the third berry. I knelt by the little bush, thanking God for the reminders I had needed so desperately.

I was still kneeling by the bush when my boys noticed me and splashed out of their pool and ran to me. "What'd you find, Mama?" the oldest one asked, curious.

"I found a promise from God," I said reverently. The boys stared for a moment and then ran back to their pool.

I decided to move the raspberry bush to a safer location, but an afternoon thunderstorm interrupted my plans. *Tomorrow I'll move my hug from God to a safer spot*, I decided. But the next morning when I walked outside to move the raspberry bush, it was gone. Not even a dried-up stalk remained to mark its existence. I was disappointed, for I wanted to keep the bush and share its fruits with others, telling them about God's special hug when I needed it so much. Then I realized that God was telling me to keep that hug in my heart to share with those who need to be encouraged and reassured that He really does care for us and knows our needs.

Raspberries are still one of my favorite fruits, and I occasionally buy them. But somehow they just don't taste as good as those three berries that grew on a bush in the middle of the garden path many years ago.

Charlotte Ishkanian is editor of the mission quarterlies and Inside Stories. *She enjoys photographing God's wonders around her and listening to people's stories of faith.*

Fellowship

Sisters

Love must be sincere. Hate what is evil;
cling to what is good. . . . Honor one another above yourselves.
—Romans 12:9, 10, NIV

As the parent of an only child, I would often hear my daughter, Brooke, regularly ask—almost plead—for siblings. Having grown up with eight brothers and sisters myself, I would often tell her how much more privileged she was to have no one with whom she had to share a bed or a room or a back seat or even clothing. I graphically laid out to her all my tales of woe, such as having to squeeze in the back seat of our family's Rambler station wagon between my sisters Julie and Marionette, complaining about how their thighs were touching mine. This was deadly, you know.

Still, my horror stories of waiting in line behind six sisters and brothers to get into the only bathroom or wearing hand-me-downs didn't seem to frighten Brooke at all. She was still convinced that having sisters would be the supreme joy of her existence.

Well, God granted Brooke the desires of her heart in a rather unconventional way. I took on the position of freshman women's dean. She suddenly had 250 sisters, each with her own needs as urgent as hers and of no less importance. Who would have thought someone else could be as upset about the shade of her nail polish or outraged by the fact that there was no H&M clothing store in Huntsville, Alabama? She could now blend her voice with others shrieking in terror as raindrops fell on their freshly coifed hair. And she had to stand in line for attention as mother spent time in the dean's office, with students who were happy, sad, sick, and every other condition in between. Also, there were young women camped out in her home at all hours of the day and night. Just as I had begun to think that this only child was starting to have a change of heart about that sibling thing, an event took place that served to prove the opposite.

The opportunity to interact lovingly with young women from a myriad of backgrounds is a gift for which I'm thankful.

We were nearing the end of an especially exhausting week when I received a call from my brother-in-law telling me my nephew had been shot. Needless to say, the report was met with hysteria, and I rushed to the hospital, leaving my daughter and niece at the dorm. I called from the hospital to see if the girls were OK, and my daughter announced that the night deans, RAs, and some other students had come to pray with them.

My nephew recovered, praise God, but the fact that girls who were not born into our family would align themselves with us like family and stop everything to rush to the aid and comfort of my daughter and niece was a true reflection of love. The opportunity to interact lovingly with young women from a myriad of backgrounds is a gift for which I'm thankful. These relationships have spawned close ties. The time I spend nurturing others yields the same posture of nurturing in them; young women to nurture others.

If I've learned one thing through this experience in "higher education," it's that life is all about relationships, and relationships are often formed in ways that many would think unlikely. I once had to confiscate the cell phones of two young women in worship. If looks could kill and if teen fury were lethal, I would not have been around to write this story. But days later when these two girls were in a situation of extreme need and I eagerly went to their rescue, one of them asked me why I would do so after the way she had behaved. I simply responded, "Because I love you." When everything else falls apart, meaningful, genuine relationships remain. That is why investing in relationships is so essential. I've made that the priority. The students and I have laughed, cried, mourned, and rejoiced together in the residence hall.

And so my daughter's craving for the companionship of "sisters" was valid. In my work I teach the young women that we *are* our sisters' keepers. We are to love and help one another— even those who may initially brace up at the mere thought of having the dean help them because, after all, they're 18 and know more than I do. I could go on about students with whom I've had a rocky start but a happy end. Again, it's all about relationships.

> In my work I teach the young women that we are our sisters' keepers. We are to love and help one another.

And how we form relationships with others reveals the characteristics of our ultimate relationship, you know, the one with our heavenly Father. Before I knew God as the ruler of the universe and my life, I often did the right thing because I didn't want to disappoint my mother—because of my love for her. Similarly, some of the young women have been honest enough to tell me that the reason they didn't break the rules is that they didn't want to disappoint me. Humbling.

I suspect love has something to do with it too. I learned that our relationship with God is much the same. He said, "If you love me, you will keep my commandments" (John 14:15, ESV). Therefore, I hope to form relationships with my students that may lead them to form a closer one with God. However, while my ultimate goal is for them to form a relationship with Jesus that is rooted in love, I'm just happy they desire to do right. That's a great, essential start to a greater end. For now, the important thing is that we have been made a family. So despite how odd the circumstances or strange my desire to share with 250 other girls, I will trust in the Lord who gave my daughter sisters.

Linda R. Anderson is residential life coordinator for freshman women at Oakwood University. As director of Carter Hall, she assists young women in their transition toward independence. She is the proud mother of a vivacious daughter, Brooke, who is a student at the university. Linda is also a public speaker and published author of the devotional book Fragments.

Drawn by Love

*Let your light so shine before men, . . .
and glorify your Father which is in heaven.*
—Matthew 5:16

In 1991, after teaching in Seventh-day Adventist schools for 17 years, I began teaching third grade in a Laurel, Maryland, public school. I had been so committed to my career as an Adventist schoolteacher that I felt I was abandoning God's work when I left the Adventist school system. I had always desired for God to use me to impact children spiritually in my work, and I questioned whether I could do this in public school.

However, I now realize that God had another plan for my life. On the first day of school at Oaklands Elementary a cute little girl walked into my classroom and melted my heart. Each day before and after school this bright-eyed third grader would find her way to me to help me prepare my classroom for instruction. Even after she left my class to advance to higher grades, she continued to return to my classroom to help out in any way she could.

Unknown to me at the time were the serious challenges my little student was facing every day in her home. I later learned that one of the reasons she would make her way back to my classroom before and after school was to find the quiet, peaceful place she didn't have at home.

After she began middle school and I transferred to another public school, we lost contact with each other. But this little girl's spirit remained with me, and I never forgot her until we reunited shortly after her high school graduation. She then told me the story of her efforts to find me. I should stop here and let my former third grader take over the story and tell you in her own words how Christ used my public school classroom to influence her to accept Jesus as her Savior and become a member of the Seventh-day Adventist Church.

Shayla speaks:

After losing contact with Mrs. Dent, I began a six-year search to find her. As her third-grade student, I knew she loved me unconditionally, and that was something I lacked in my life as a child. While talking with a group of friends in the principal's office at Laurel High School and comparing stories of our favorite teachers, I mentioned Judy Dent's name and was overheard by a secretary in the office. To my surprise, the secretary recognized her name and helped me find the one person who had made such a positive impression on my life.

As her third-grade student, I knew she loved me unconditionally, and that was something I lacked in my life as a child.

Several years after finding Mrs. Dent, whenever I had a free Sabbath I would surprise her and join her for worship at Emmanuel Brinklow Seventh-day Adventist Church. On one surprise visit I spent Sabbath with her family at a time in my life when I was once again searching for rest and peace.

On February 19, 2010, Judy Dent's birthday, the Lord confirmed that I needed to move. I told God, "I hear You, Lord. I trust You to guide me." That evening after leaving the Dents' home, I received a call from Mrs. Dent. "Shayla, I need you to prepare to come to our home to live." She said her husband approved and that they wanted me to be able to focus on finishing college. She said, "So please pray about it." I stopped her in my tears. She did not know I had already asked God that same day to help me find a place to live!

After moving into the Dents' home, I came to understand that Sunday is not the Bible Sabbath. Friday night worships and Sabbath afternoon discussions led to my desire to have Bible studies. I felt as though I was not growing spiritually, and I simply wanted to know and do God's will for my life.

One Friday evening on my way home, I talked with God. I felt convicted that I needed to become a Sabbathkeeper. I then decided to follow Christ all the way. On September 17, 2011, I took my stand to be baptized into the Seventh-day Adventist Church.

My journey in becoming a born-again Christian in the Seventh-day Adventist Church is directly related to the relationship I was blessed to have with my third-grade public school teacher who lived out her beliefs before me and her other students. We have all had our share of fires in life. I have certainly had mine, but God always comes through in His time. There is no doubt in my mind that it was God who placed Mrs. Dent in my life when I was a child in order to draw me nearer to Him and the Bible truth of the seventh-day Sabbath.

Judy B. Dent, recently retired public school teacher and principal, writes from Brandywine, Maryland. She enjoys nature walks, singing, and lifting up the name of Jesus.

A Hot Meal and a Smile

Withhold not good from them to whom it is due,
when it is in the power of thine hand to do it.
—Proverbs 3:27

I was a teenager when I first heard the saying "There but for the grace of God go I." It impacted me profoundly because I instantly recognized that it is only because of God's grace that I am spared specific experiences and circumstances in my life. One such circumstance that has always triggered strong emotions in me is the threat of being homeless. The grim specter of pervasive homelessness rocks our society today. Statistically most of us are within one or two paychecks away from being in a position where everything we have worked for could be taken from us. And if we are truthful, if we lost our jobs and steady flow of income, many of us could easily be on a downhill slide toward being in a place where we are no longer safe in the comforts of our own homes. Without familial support or the support of good friends, it is not inconceivable that we could be in a position where we are living in our cars, in a shelter, or on the streets. It is important to remember that most people who are homeless are so because of circumstances, not by choice.

Long before it was politically correct to be concerned about the homeless population of our urban cities, the pastor of my church started a program called Operation Hope, which reached out to the homeless population of Decatur, Georgia. Every night the church doors were open to the men of the community, and they could find a safe refuge, a good meal, a hot shower, and a bed for the night. Insurance concerns eventually shut down that program, but the mantel of at least providing a meal for the homeless community was picked up, and for more than 20 years every Sabbath morning a group of dedicated men and women gather at 3:00 a.m. and prepare food to feed an average of 750 men and women at two local shelters. Every Sabbath. The meal is not fancy—scrambled eggs, grits, hash browns, bread and juice—but it is hearty, hot, and served with a smile.

It isn't always easy hearing the alarm go off at 2:30 on Sabbath morning, but my impetus is the knowledge that somehow, through my efforts, people are fed and God is glorified.

It is a blessing for my mother and me to participate in this weekly program. It isn't always easy hearing the alarm go off at 2:30 on Sabbath morning, but my impetus is the knowledge that somehow, through my efforts, people are fed and God is glorified. I am a big believer in the biblical mandate "to whom much is given, much is required" (see Luke 12:48). I am blessed beyond measure with a job that provides a steady income to provide not only for my needs but a lot of my wants and desires as well. Getting up early in the morning to cook, something that I love to do anyway, is no true hardship.

I don't personally go downtown to help serve the food at the shelters, but I know that the people in the shelters are blessed each week because of the faithfulness shown by the people who show up to cook the food, as well as by those who go mingle with and touch the people in the shelters. It is not for me to understand or judge what happened in someone's life that landed him or her in a shelter, whether the person's dependence on the shelter is temporary or seemingly permanent. It may not even be my mission to change their circumstances. That is all within God's plan for their lives . . . and mine.

Often we think of stewardship as being only about money—you know, the faithful return of our tithes and the giving of a liberal offering. In our ministry to the homeless population, I am learning that stewardship is also about returning your time, talents, and skills. In Matthew 25, beginning with verse 34, we are shown a scene of Jesus speaking to His saints. After pronouncing His judgment, He tells one group that He is rewarding them for their stewardship toward others: "You clothed Me, fed Me, visited with Me; enter into the kingdom." The group of saints is astounded and says, "When did we do all that?" God's response: "Every time you did it for your brothers and sisters, you did it for Me." I may never meet any of the people who benefited directly from this ministry and whose lives may have been changed because I got up early on a Sabbath morning. All I have to do is show up, cook up some eggs, and trust that God will use that act of faithfulness to bless someone else as He sees fit. I am happy just to be a small part of the process, and I trust that God will use my small act of faithfulness to do great things for His glory.

> In our ministry to the homeless population, I am learning that stewardship is also about returning your time, talents, and skills.

Kristina Smith is a legal secretary in Atlanta, Georgia, who recently published her first book, Thoughts From God's Favorite Child. *She is thrilled to be included with all the other wonderful women of God who have contributed to this book.*

Of Neighbors and Friends

Thou shalt love thy neighbour as thyself.
—Matthew 22:39

Knock-knock! The door opened. "Hi, my name's Carol. I live upstairs. Please forgive me if my piano playing disturbed you." (I had heard through the grapevine that someone was playing the piano "very loud.") "Please accept these flowers, and I am so sorry."

Standing in the doorway was a very pleasant-looking woman. She introduced herself. "I'm Dolly. No, I didn't complain. Come in." Thus began one of the most exciting, funniest, enjoyable friendships I could ever imagine, with Dolly and her husband, Eddie.

I was forever in and out of their apartment. They were my family. We ate together, sorrowed together, laughed together, and loved each other.

We ate the best pizza, at their special place. We munched on that huge onion ring thing together, at their special place. We took drives to the mall and laughed so hard as we watched Dolly get in one of those self-driving carts, backing up and ramming into things. Of course, Eddie "didn't know us." So many things we did together. Wonderful neighbors! A grand friendship!

They were always helping people. Lois was one of those people. Quiet and shy, she lived with them. The four of us had marvelous times in their apartment.

Dolly had stopped going to her church for various reasons. Eddie was still attending his church. Lois didn't have any church affiliation. Eddie was a Sunday school teacher. I would give him religious books to read, and he would use them in his class.

One summer Dolly's granddaughter came to visit for the entire summer. Eddie took her to church. She loved it. Dolly started attending with the two of them. They all loved church. When the summer ended, Dolly's granddaughter returned home, and Eddie and Dolly continued attending church.

Stopping by their apartment one evening, Dolly was frantically turning the pages of her Bible. Dolly loved reading her Bible; the pages were worn and torn. Growing up, she was never allowed to touch a Bible, much less read it or have one of her own.

I was forever in and out of their apartment. They were my family. We ate together, sorrowed together, laughed together, and loved each other.

"Sister"—she always called me that—"where is the book of Paul?"

"Paul?" I asked with a smile.

"Yes, Paul. Where do I find Paul?"

"Dolly, there's no book in the Bible called Paul. Tell me what you are looking for."

She told me. I sat down and, taking her worn Bible in hand, found the book that pertained to the subject she was interested in. That was the beginning of many conversations we had about things she learned at church, read in the Bible, and what she had been taught as a child. Dolly was seeking answers and eager to gain understanding.

On one of my many visits to their apartment I asked Eddie, Dolly, and Lois if they would like to study the Bible. They agreed. Dolly had her Bible, Eddie had his, and I bought Lois one. We began using a simple Bible lesson designed to help you get all the answers from reading the Bible. There were many questions and statements: *I can pray to Mary, and she will tell Jesus what I need. When you die, you go to heaven. Where is Jesus? You mean, pork is out?* We'd open the Bible, find the text, and get the answers. They were satisfied. I watched the Holy Spirit illuminate the minds of Dolly, Eddie, and Lois and lovingly change their lives.

For me, it all boils down to being faithful to the trust Jesus has given me and being like Him.

Dolly wore expensive jewelry. When I visited her one day, she said, "Sister, I was putting on my earrings, and someone said to me, 'One day you will exchange them for a crown.' Who was that?"

"That Someone," I said, "is the Holy Spirit speaking to you." And the earrings came off, along with all the other jewelry.

Sadly, Dolly had cancer and other health challenges. I went to see her one day, and she was very concerned over a toe that was not healing and turning gangrenous. She said, "Sister, I've put holy water on it, but it's not working."

"Dolly," I said, "let's ask Jesus to heal it." I prayed a simple prayer of faith for the healing of Dolly's toe and thanked Him. A few days later I dropped by and Dolly was beside herself: "Sister, what the holy water couldn't do, Jesus did!"

Because God's providence led me to their apartment and the start of a special friendship, Dolly, Eddie, and Lois were baptized in Christ in the Seventh-day Adventist Church.

Eddie and Lois have moved to different states now and remain faithful to Jesus. And Dolly, my dear sister, is resting in the grave, waiting for her Savior to call her in the first resurrection. How they have touched my life!

I have discovered that stewardship is a lifestyle that encompasses many things: friendship, finances, kindness, hospitality, generosity; the list goes on and on.

For me, it all boils down to being faithful to the trust Jesus has given me and being like Him. As the words of a song state: "Be like Jesus, this my song, in the home and in the throng; be like Jesus all day long! I would be like Jesus."

Carol Barron, who totally enjoys life, Jesus, and her adult children, writes from Silver Spring, Maryland.

Finance

Trusting His Promises

But seek first the kingdom of God and His righteousness,
and all these things shall be added to you.
—Matthew 6:33, NKJV

I like to know. As a planner, I find it important to have the "how, when, and where" of things established, not only to ensure that everything goes smoothly but also to give me my own peace of mind. So when something occurs that is out of sync with what has been set in place, it can potentially become a catalyst for confusion and sometimes fear, both of which create unwanted stress. I find this to be especially true in the area of finances.

As a single female who at times feels overworked and underpaid, I am often disconcerted when unexpected expenses arise. What happens when the car breaks down right before payday? The realization that I'll receive a paycheck in a couple of days is comforting. *Hallelujah! Praise the Lord! I'll be able to take my car to the mechanic for repair.* The question is, do I pay the mechanic with tithe money or do I return my tithe, then pay the mechanic, knowing I won't have money left to cover my regular expenses? How am I going to meet all of my financial demands if I return tithe *and* pay the mechanic?

On many occasions I've wanted to use my tithe money for other expenses such as emergency repairs, putting a little extra toward a bill, or even doing a mini home "makeover" by purchasing a new piece of furniture. I, in my finite wisdom, didn't always understand why the tithe is so important. *Really, Lord? I have the money right now to do what I need to do; it's the exact amount, even. You mean I have to give this up first and then wait to take care of whatever the pressing matter at hand is?* God's response is "Yes." *But why, Lord?* (As I said before, I like to know.) Fortunately, God understands folks like me and gives His answer in His Word: "Bring all the tithes into the storehouse, that there may be food in My house" (Mal. 3:10, NKJV).

> The question is, do I pay the mechanic with tithe money or do I return my tithe, then pay the mechanic, knowing I won't have money left to cover my regular expenses?

I've heard, read, and recited this passage many times, but applying it is not always so simple. The scripture makes sense. *I am here to serve You, and I do that in a practical way by helping to support mission work and other projects.* Still I ask, "Why, Lord?" And again, the Lord helps me understand: "Will a man rob God? Yet you have robbed Me! But you say, 'In what way have we robbed You?' In tithes and offerings" (Mal. 3:8, 9, NKJV).

Ouch! In this passage the Lord not only addresses our priorities but also makes it clear that the money we've been given comes from Him. Yes, it's important to take care of financial responsibilities, but it's more important to be faithful stewards. The word "entrust" speaks of stewardship. The Lord of heaven and earth actually *trusts* us to be good stewards of all that He gives us. Now, if God trusts me enough to be faithful with His money and tithe 10 percent, how is it that my trust in Him suddenly falters when I consider giving Him back only 10 percent of the 100 percent that is rightfully His?

We often trust our employers more than God to provide our financial needs. God's love and provision are unchanging; He asks for only 10 percent, while many places of business add on a 15, 20, and sometimes 30 percent gratuity. My experience has been that God's blessings are far greater. Indeed, He is "able to do exceeding abundantly above all that we ask or think" (Eph. 3:20).

The confusion, fear, and stress seem ridiculous when I look at it in these terms. When God says that He will supply all our needs, He means it. Sometimes it's difficult for us single women to grasp this when we observe what's going on around us. We have friends who are married, which often means theirs is a two-income household. But God's Word doesn't say that He knows the number of hairs on only a married woman's head; that verse includes all of us.

I'll give you an example. Remember the furniture I mentioned earlier? Well, it was time for me to replace a well-worn, literally coming-apart-at-the-seams couch that I'd had for years. The couch I wanted to purchase was completely out of my budget. After returning my tithe, giving an offering, and paying my bills, there's not much left for big-ticket items such as furniture. But here is how God works. I was on my way to the laundry room at my complex when my neighbor saw me and stopped me to say that she was buying new furniture and wanted to know if I would like to have her couch! I could barely believe my ears, and then when I saw what she was offering me, I was amazed. The couch was practically brand-new and in my favorite style! I have so many more stories like this.

I have found that being a good steward of God's money is not about whether or not I'll know how, when, and where I'll have the means to make ends meet. It's about my trust in God's promises to me.

Julie Bryan writes from Los Angeles, California, and enjoys filmmaking and travel.

I Do

Where no counsel is, the people fall:
but in the multitude of counsellors there is safety.
—Proverbs 11:14

Last spring I entered into the biggest commitment of my life thus far. For months I prepped and prayed and planned, and then on the first day of May I signed on the dotted line—actually, countless dotted lines!—and became a first-time homeowner.

Early on in the process, I, as a single woman, realized that selecting and purchasing a home is actually quite similar to that "other" major life event: getting married. Although an (in my case) aluminum siding structure cannot be compared to a living, breathing, life partner, much of the guidance I received and knowledge I gained along the way to my new home is applicable to both endeavors. Since "rushing into things" would be a grievous error in either situation, I thought I would share with you my recent experience and what it taught me, in hopes that it will be helpful, and perhaps even encouraging, to other women considering *either* big step.

Seek God Above All Things

Sixteenth-century friar Paschal Baylon wrote, "It is right for you to seek God before and above everything else, because the majesty of God wishes you to receive what you ask for." I would echo this counsel when undertaking *any* major decision. It was certainly key to my confidence, clarity, and peace of mind last spring, and I'm positive it is integral to successful marital matches as well.

Is the choice to make such an expensive commitment on a single salary and in an uncertain economy the right one? Should I dip into my retirement savings account to boost my initial down payment? Do I pass on a house after my offer was outbid, or do I extend my price range a few thousand dollars? All of these matters I placed before God in prayer.

More than anyone else or even yourself, God loves you and wants the best for you. Make every step of the process a matter of prayer, and He will lead you in the way that you should go, to an outcome that is right for your circumstances.

"Be not controlled by the desire for wealth, the dictates of fashion, or the customs of society. Consider what will tend most to simplicity, purity, health, and real worth" (*The Adventist Home*, p. 131).

Be Patient and Consider the Advice of Others

Most of my friends and family already own their own homes. Did that make me envious or feel like I was being left behind? Sometimes. More often it motivated me to forgo the cute new shoes in lieu of a few more dollars in my house fund. It also made these individuals the perfect source of information!

Proverbs 15:22 cautions, "Plans fail for lack of counsel, but with many advisers they succeed" (NIV). The two years prior to my purchase were spent not only saving money but also educating myself by way of my parents, my friends, a loan officer, and, of course, the Internet. This was going to be the biggest commitment of my life thus far, and I wanted to get it right! That's sage advice for those pondering a lifetime commitment to a piece of property *or* another human being.

Taking into consideration the knowledge and experience of others does not imply that you do not trust God fully or yourself enough. It simply means that you are wise enough to recognize resources when they are right in front of you.

Reality Versus Fairy Tale

"The gospel . . . teaches us to estimate things at their true value, and to give the most effort to the things of greatest worth—the things that will endure. This lesson is needed by those upon whom rests the responsibility of selecting a home. . . . Be not controlled by the desire for wealth, the dictates of fashion, or the customs of society. Consider what will tend most to simplicity, purity, health, and real worth" (*The Adventist Home*, p. 131).

Early on in the process, I, as a single woman, realized that selecting and purchasing a home is actually quite similar to that "other" major life event: getting married

Much like the prospective bride, I started my search for "the one" with a wish list. I wanted outdoor space, nearby running trails, covered parking, room for out-of-town guests . . . the list went on and on. Unfortunately, my bank account did not.

After a few trips out with a very patient real estate agent, I realized that I needed to refocus on needs, not wants. Security, accessibility, resale value, and minimal upkeep quickly became much more important than a trendy zip code and vaulted ceilings.

I did not compromise, by any means, but I chose with my head *as well as* my heart.

As a single woman in her mid-30s, signing a 30-year mortgage was not a decision I made lightly, nor should it have been. But with my first year of payments behind me, my car parked safely away from the elements in the garage, and my bedroom freshly painted the perfect shade of blue, I know it was the right one for me.

Melissa Reid is the associate editor of Liberty *magazine and the executive director of the North American Religious Liberty Association, a member-driven advocacy organization dedicated to the cause of religious freedom.*

He Never Fails

And they that know thy name will put their trust in thee:
for thou, Lord, hast not forsaken them that seek thee.
—Psalm 9:10

Faith is a firm reliance on the integrity, ability, or character of a person or thing. When we talk about faith, it is not a book experience. It is about a relationship with the God of the universe, about trusting Him when we cannot see Him, and about knowing that He is truly concerned for us and what affects us. God can, and will, handle anything that crosses our path on this earthly journey.

I believe that real trust is not developed on sunny days. For it is when darkness overwhelms our lives that we are compelled to trust that the Son is behind the cloud and will shine through for us at the time that is best for us.

Not seeing and yet believing. Why is it so easy for us to have faith in temporal things and question the spiritual? Because we experience the world primarily through our senses, we want to see things; we want to be able to touch things. In my experience I have found that faith is like walking into an empty dark room, begging for help, and receiving the help needed. Because Jesus is the reason for faith, He is the foundation. Faith is not a book experience; it is a personal, day-by-day experience with Jesus Christ.

God entrusted me with two loving children, and being a faithful steward of their upbringing and education was always important to me. Sending my children to Seventh-day Adventist schools was my goal, a precious legacy that my parents passed on to me. Though it was always a financial challenge, as I lived from paycheck to paycheck, my faith in God supplied the oil that put the wheels in motion.

God entrusted me with two loving children, and being a faithful steward of their upbringing and education was always important to me.

On one occasion during the children's summer break, I simply did not see how I could continue sending them to an Adventist school. I decided to enroll them in a Christian school right across the road from where I was living. I could see no other alternative. It was a good school with a good reputation. However, my nights were filled with uneasiness. Nevertheless, I knew public school was not an option. As the first day of the school year drew near, I began to prepare my two children for this change in schools. What could they do but trust their mother's decision? When I discussed my decision with my family members, they prayed with me and reminded me that the Lord would direct my path. These were His children, and I had to know without a doubt where He wanted them to attend school.

No tug at the heart can be greater than one that has to do with the welfare and best interests of your children. Doubts flooded my mind. Although I reviewed the education program at this Christian establishment, I wondered if my children would be taught something that was contrary to our Seventh-day Adventist beliefs and if they would be strong enough to stand for what they had been taught according to the Bible.

To back up a bit, weeks before I enrolled my sweet youngsters, a special leader who was preparing to attend Andrews University had advised me to keep my faith strong. Thinking back to his encouragement, I hesitantly, and with much trepidation, decided against the convenient Christian school across the road and enrolled them in the Adventist school instead. I can't say that the days surrounding my new decision and leading up to the first day of school I had no anxiety as to where the funds would come from. The thought of once again paying Adventist school fees was overwhelming as I drove to the school with nothing more than a meager check in hand and a promise to pay the monthly tuition. But I had learned to have faith in God because He had come through before and He always follows through on His promises.

I have learned that faithful stewardship involves trusting God in spite of how daunting a situation might seem. When we desire to honor Him, He honors us and reveals Himself in ways we never imagined.

Several weeks went by, and one day, in the mail, was a letter from this promising leader and his wife stating that they had prayed about my situation and would send a check each month toward my children's tuition fees. Keep in mind that they had little or no salary; in choosing to assist with the monthly school bill, they chose to put themselves on the line. I became aware of their decision only *after* I had already made the step of faith and enrolled my children in our church school. That was a miracle! I decided if *they* could make that commitment, I had to do the same and keep my children enrolled in a Seventh-day Adventist school. This experience as a whole is where my faith journey began and was strengthened.

I have learned that faithful stewardship involves trusting God in spite of how daunting or impossible a situation might seem. When we desire to honor Him, He honors us and reveals Himself in ways we never imagined.

Praise God! Both of my children achieved academic success; one serves in our Adventist educational system, and the other has contributed to our government.

Marialyce Fordham is a prayer warrior and freelance writer who enjoys nature walks and spending time with her five grandchildren. She lives in Laurel, Maryland.

I Am That Steward

For thy Maker is thine husband;
the Lord of hosts is his name.
—Isaiah 54:5

In the year that my husband, Kenny, died, I found my Isaiah 54 Husband. Now, 16 years later, I have discovered that when He gave me His word, "For I am the Lord, I change not" (Mal. 3:6), He sincerely meant it. For that always-faithful Friend has proved Himself to be my counselor, companion, peace speaker, deliverer, and so much more.

It was no wonder, then, that I was calmer than most when, four years ago, my red-faced manager served me the proverbial pink slip. Initially I neither panicked nor complained. I was certain that this Husband and Provider of mine had the perfect job lined up for me. However, every relationship has to be tested, and for any marriage to survive, there has to be mutual trust. I knew that I could trust Him, but could He trust that when the relationship was thrust into stormy waters, I would not jump ship? Could He trust me to keep my end of the bargain, to make my financial contributions of one tenth, and then some to the household budget?

One of the main stressors in many marriages is finances, and ours would be no different. The first two years of joblessness went by smoothly, and I remained faithful to my commitment to contribute financially. I remember boasting at every opportunity to anyone who would listen how my God-husband was keeping His end of His bargain. Through His loving providence, I was still receiving income from various sources. Additionally, my mortgage payments were temporarily reduced; I received a substantial check for moneys owed me, utilities were taken care of, food was never scarce, and, at His promptings, I was able to share my tangible blessings with others. Actually, my situation was as though I still had a job. My commitment to financial stewardship was alive and well. How could I not trust Him?

As long as the bills were being paid and there was food on the table, I could love and trust Him.

Days turned into weeks and weeks into months of constant dialogue between us. Then, in the third year, without warning, communication on His end stopped, and He became seemingly invisible. This period of silence strangely coincided with the depletion of one of my major sources of income, and the bills kept coming. I continued to faithfully contribute until my initial mortgage amount was reinstated. That is when trust disappeared and fear appeared. So, regrettably, I cheated on Him by having an affair with that thieving Mr. Panic. I robbed my Husband/Provider in order to pay my mortgage provider. My fidelity to stewardship was anemic and on life support. My treasured peace was stolen. My foolish decision was only a temporary financial fix. Our relationship was in trouble. "Lord, are You there?" The familiar ring of His voice was gone, obscured by worry. What a price to pay! I now know that even when I am not aware of His presence, the reality is that He is always there. He never stopped loving. When I was unfaithful, He remained faithful. Homelessness loomed, the pantry was bare, the piggy bank was empty, yet I never missed a meal. As He had promised, He never changed!

My new Husband, I learned, loves to send me God winks, those special reassurances. I discovered how intimately He knew me by watching Him turn my passion for dogs and the joy that they bring me into a thriving home business. It was as though the windows of heaven opened up; dogs—big dogs, small dogs, blind dogs, dogs in Pampers—just came pouring down. I was smiling again.

He winked again, and my mortgage payments were reduced by half. Did He walk into the mortgage company and demand this, or did He telephone the chief financial officer and personally arrange it just for me? However He did it, it was done! He was working behind the scenes all along. If only I was as patient as He was.

He trusts us enough to partner with Him in managing His resources for the benefit of others and to rid us of our natural tendencies to be covetous and selfish.

Yet another wink. This efficient, long-range planner knew from our earlier discussions that babysitting was not an option. What did He do? He set me up! He sent me twin babies to care for, not canine babies, but human babies, Pampers and all. And just in time. It turned out that this was His way of preparing me for a surprise job, one that I now hold as an educator to children with needs similar to my babies'. This experience was a big boost. Trust was restored.

My stewardship relationship with Him is revived. I am cheerfully returning the tenth. I am still playing catch up with other obligations, but I am happy!

Can this partnership survive? Can He now trust me to do my

part? Yes, because of what I have learned from the unfailing love and boundless grace of this amazing God-husband. This wonderful Owner of the thousand hills on which His cattle graze had me in mind when He introduced this financial plan with benefits. So, with our daily renewal of vows, He can trust me to, unselfishly and without covetousness, manage His resources to serve others. And how do we both benefit? He gets my wholehearted commitment, and I get His promised peace, joy, and support. Now I can rest with quiet confidence in His "love that wilt not let me go." In Luke 12:43 Jesus pronounced a blessing on the faithful steward. By faith *I* am that steward.

Kathleen "Kay" Murrell is a resident of Maryland and is currently working in New York in the field of special education.

Fitness

Get Up, Girl!

Wherefore he saith, Awake thou that sleepest,
and arise from the dead,
and Christ shall give thee light.
—Ephesians 5:14

I often chuckle when I read Ephesians 5:14, as if the Lord Himself is saying, "Gina, get up from that bed and allow Me to give you light!" With the demands of an extremely heavy work schedule, there never seem to be enough hours in the day to complete tasks. There are demands from family members about things apparently only *I* can handle, demands from friends who need a listening ear. The list of demands seem to persist on and on.

As a health educator, I've learned that it's not enough to be a "good" steward of my health; I must be a "great" steward so that the life I live will be an example of God's grace toward me. How in the world does the Lord expect me to exercise and eat right, not just to be a "good" steward, but a "great" steward of my health, and yet get all of these other tasks completed? Even Jesus said, "Come away . . . and rest a while" (Mark 6:31, ESV). It seems that He clearly understood our need for rest and relaxation. Getting up early to have worship already takes a toll on my few remaining hours, yet I feel compelled to exercise. How in the world am I to complete all of this in a mere 24 hours?

Well, I've found that there are several things that I can do to assist in the endeavor of exercising and eating right. First of all, as a great steward, I must plan. I have to plan to manage my time as well as plan *what* I need to get done. This planning moves from the wide sphere of each task that needs to be completed that day to the small innuendos of the amount and type of exercise that I'm doing that day and what I'm going to eat that day. And while I hate journaling, I have learned that when I write down what I have eaten that day, it allows me to be a better steward by helping me control my intake the next day.

As a health educator, I've learned that it's not enough to be a "good" steward of my health; I must be a "great" steward so that the life I live will be an example of God's grace toward me.

I have also learned that in order to be a "great" steward, I've got to start "early, mid-, and late." That's sounds like an oxymoron, but it's not. I've got to start out early with morning worship, for I have found that without proper worship, nothing else is completed. I've found that having worship *first* puts everything in proper perspective for the day. The "mid-" function means that I ask God's guidance before embarking on every task throughout the day. This allows Christ to keep me focused through the day. The "late" function means that before I go to bed, I've got to have worship *again*. This is the only thing that is going to give me enough strength to start this process all over again the next morning. I've also found that God is honest, meaning that if I spend "too much" time in worship, He'll give it back to me.

I've discovered that with a hectic schedule and the demands of life, women often have a hard time putting themselves first, but I've learned that if I live healthfully and take care of myself first, I have so much more to offer to those who are in my sphere of influence. When I eat right, exercise daily, and plan well, everyone wins. As I review the text in Ephesians 5:14, I note that God doesn't stop where He tells me to "arise." Ephesians 5 continues to say, "So be careful how you live. Don't live like fools, but like those who are wise. Make the most of every opportunity in these evil days. Don't act thoughtlessly, but understand what the Lord wants you to do" (verses 15–17, NLT).

I'm so glad that the Lord tells me that after I've done "all" (the cleaning, the cooking, the writing, the bill paying, the driving, the grocery shopping, the healing of the sick, and the raising of the dead), I can just "stand" (Eph. 6:13).

He tells me that His grace is sufficient for me and that His strength is made perfect in weakness (2 Cor. 12:9). Lord, have mercy! I feel weak every morning, but I continue to remember, "The Sovereign Lord is my strength; he makes my feet like the feet of a deer, he enables me to tread on the heights" (Hab. 3:19, NIV).

He continues to give me the ability to run and to eat right. He continues to allow my body to be *His* temple, for *His* glory, so that I can ultimately see *His* face.

I've discovered that with a hectic schedule and the demands of life, women often have a hard time putting themselves first, but I've learned that if I live healthfully and take care of myself first, I have so much more to offer to those who are in my sphere of influence.

Gina Brown *writes from Bowie, Maryland, and enjoys her work as an associate professor at Loma Linda University immensely. The highlight of every day is spending time with her family.*

Living Bodies, Living Foods: The Choice Is Yours

I will praise thee; for I am fearfully and wonderfully made:
marvellous are thy works; and that my soul knoweth right well.
—Psalm 139:14

What started as a personal experiment turned into a seven-year passion as I have journeyed the road of discovering raw foods and their benefits. In the spring of 2005, along with a group of my close friends, I embarked on a 21-day juicing and cleansing diet.

Each one of us did this for different reasons. Some dreamed about getting into their swimsuit before a summer beach vacation. Others, feeling stressed and unable to cope with the demands of everyday living, looked for the promised energy increase, improved sleep, clearer thinking, and better concentration. Yet others, dealing with a particular health challenge, hoped for a cure. Each of us had different reasons for staying on the program, and in some way we all benefited from the results.

During the cleansing and follow-up portion of this diet, we were to use only organic fruits and vegetables in order to get a maximum of nutrients. Plenty of pure, living spring water was also a must, to ensure removal of toxins and products of metabolic waste. (You can find a free spring water supply in your area by going to www. findaspring.com.)

I recall my friends who took part in that adventure proudly displaying their thinner bodies, glowing skin, improved health, increased energy, and a more positive attitude.

Although many of us found it hard to stay on the program for the entire 21 days, the diet enabled us to change our eating habits. Some of us never went back to the way we ate before. Some included more fruits and vegetables in their diet. Others may have fallen off the wagon but have never forgotten how to go back and reclaim the state and feeling of well-being.

During this process I felt compelled to find out more about superfoods (such as goji berries, noni fruit, mangosteen, maca root, cacao beans, sea vegetables, marine phytoplankton, coconut oil, and spirulina) and superherbs (such as holy basil, turmeric extract, mucuna, rose hips, horsetail, stinging nettles, and gingko biloba). I wanted to share with others how to strengthen and beautify their bodies.

I recall my friends who took part in that adventure proudly displaying their thinner bodies, glowing skin, improved health, increased energy, and more positive attitude.

In the winter of 2009 I enrolled in the David "Avocado" Wolfe's Ultimate Raw Nutrition Certification program, offered by the BodyMind Institute in Alberta, Canada. In December 2011 I completed the curriculum. I have learned how to live naturally, sustainably, and successfully in this world.

The Greek philosopher Hippocrates, who is also referred to as the father of medicine, famously said, "Let food be thy medicine and medicine be thy food." A doctor-recommended five daily servings of fruits and vegetables might be hard to consume, but throwing it all in a blender and drinking a nutritious green smoothie makes a much easier routine to follow.

In my quest for staying healthy, I continue to be curious about how I can best nourish my body. Everyone knows the saying "You are what you eat." But how many of us take it seriously and make food choices that can affect us on physical, emotional, and spiritual levels? In all aspects of life—our work, exercise program, or nutrition—the little things add up. We cannot achieve health benefits by doing something only now and then. Consistency in healthful eating, exercise, and other choices is what makes the difference.

An excellent customer service rule is based on three C's: Consistency creates credibility. How about applying this golden rule to your personal health practices? When you consistently live by sound health principles, others will notice the positive changes. Your healthful glow and increased energy will speak for themselves.

The psalmist reminds us that we are "fearfully and wonderfully made," designed by the Creator Himself. Only God could design the human body with all of its fascinating intricacies. As stewards of our bodies, we have a duty to make wise food choices in conjunction with regular exercise to help our bodies function at an optimum level.

I continue to enjoy good health, and trust that God will continue to bless me in my health practices. He wants us to live abundantly. I choose life.

Grazyna Dabrowska writes from Silver Spring, Maryland. She works in Client Care Services at Adventist Risk Management, Inc., and enjoys reading, gardening, nutrition, and exercise.

The Stewardship of the Mind

Thou wilt keep him in perfect peace,
whose mind is stayed on thee.
—Isaiah 26:3

We often think of possessions, funds, or things when it comes to stewardship, but I learned an important lesson in personal stewardship a few years ago when I decided to pursue my doctorate in educational leadership and change.

I was working as an assistant administrator of Oakwood University, directing seven departments, with the primary responsibility of managing Oakwood Memorial Gardens cemetery and the campus radio station, WJOU. Despite my position, I was still struggling financially, so I took on additional adjunct teaching positions each semester at Oakwood and the other local universities at night during the summer. I was doing all of this *and* still trying to study for my doctorate *and*—let's not forget—take care of my two children properly! I later was asked to switch positions, and became director of alumni relations for Oakwood while still running the radio station. I no longer had to deal with the emotional burials of Oakwood Memorial, but now I had to travel for the school. Oh, and let's not forget my speaking engagements on sexual abuse through Genesis Week Ministries! I quickly found myself overextended; overworked; and spiritually, mentally, and physically completely burned out.

Although my graduate school schedule was flexible and designed for working professionals, I fell behind, and each semester that I extended my work cost thousands of additional dollars. My education was at a standstill, and I was afraid that I would be removed from my program. I was anxious and terrified about my life and my future. I was literally breaking out into hives regularly, had nervous tics in my eyelids, and was not sleeping. And soon the tics began to manifest themselves down my cheek.

I quickly found myself overextended; overworked; and spiritually, mentally, and physically completely burned out.

That frightened me, so I went to a counselor and began to tell him everything that I was going through. After listening quietly, he asked me, "Vicki, do you know what a nervous breakdown is?"

I had always heard about them, but I just thought you had to do something really "crazy" to warrant the designation "nervous breakdown."

He said, "If you don't let go of something in your life immediately, I will recommend that you be hospitalized for a few weeks to prevent a complete breakdown of your nervous system."

I was stunned. "I have kids in school! I can't go to a hospital for weeks! I could even lose them if the state thinks I am unstable!" I wailed.

"If you keep going the way you are going, you may not have a choice," he replied quietly.

I knew my counselor was right, but I dreaded what I needed to do. I worked up the courage and spoke with my adviser at my school, and he suggested a leave of absence. I also made the difficult decision to ask to step down from one of my positions at Oakwood as director of alumni relations. I also reduced my time as a chorister in my church, stopped the speaking engagements, and learned a wonderful, magical word: no.

You see, I had become a very poor steward of God's precious resource—*me*. I was not caring for myself *or* my children. I was trying my best to please everyone, meet the impossible standards I had set for myself, and pretend that I was a superhero who never needed to stop or ask for help. Matthew 11:28 says, "Come to me, all you who are weary and burdened, and I will give you rest" (NIV). First Peter 5:7 says, "Cast all your anxiety on him because he cares for you" (NIV). Oh, if I had only really learned to trust Him with *all* of my resources!

You see, I had become a very poor steward of God's precious resource—me.

Won't you be a good steward with your most precious resource? As the song says: "O, what needless pain we bear!" If only we could learn to cast those cares, anxieties, and burdened, broken hearts—that heavy, needless pain—upon Jesus and learn to be true stewards of our minds. I am still learning, but true stewardship is never easy. Whenever I get overextended, I hum the sweet melody of the classic hymn "Does Jesus Care?":

> *O yes, He cares— I know He cares!*
> *His heart is touched with my grief;*
> *When the days are weary, the long nights dreary,*
> *I know my Savior cares.*

As I learned to be a better steward, I was able to focus on the task that God had given me. I completed my doctorate from Fielding Graduate University with a 4.0 average on a wonderful date: November 11, 2011 (11-11-11!). Now I am learning to steward my future plans by taking His promise to heart. "Trust in the Lord with *all* thine heart" (Prov. 3:5). I am learning to lean fully, cast carefully, lie joyfully, and rest easily in the blessed stewardship of the mind.

Victoria Joiner Miller has served at Oakwood University for more than 20 years as general manager of Praise 90.1 FM, WJOU. She is also adjunct professor of communication at Oakwood University, Alabama A&M University, and Calhoun Community College. She is the mother of two wonderful children, Jennifer, a junior at Oakwood University, and David, age 12. She is a musician and speaker and loves genealogical research. Most of all, she is a child of the King. She often says, "Not perfect—just forgiven!"

My Healer and Friend

And we know that all things work together for good to them that love
God, to them who are the called according to his purpose.
—Romans 8:28

It was a beautiful summer day. I was working at a nursing facility when I noticed a message on my cell phone from my doctor. He wanted me to call him.

My most recent mammogram had been a bit abnormal, some more tests had been done, and I was waiting for the results. I wasn't worried, because I was a lifetime vegetarian, had never smoked, didn't drink alcohol, and didn't even consume caffeine. I was a steward of my health.

Now I needed to call my physician. As he answered the call, he simply said, "I'm sorry, but your tests show you have invasive breast cancer." I was stunned. Breast cancer had never even registered on my radar. What would that mean? Hadn't I taken care of myself? Hadn't I been a good steward of my health? My mother had died a few years earlier from another form of cancer. Would this mean curtains for me, too? What would my life and future look like now?

My husband was out of town on business. I began praying for

him. Would he have to live alone? My grown children—what would this mean for them?

During my next visit with the doctor, I learned a little more. He recommended two options: a modified mastectomy (removing the entire breast) or a lumpectomy (removing only the affected part), followed by radiation treatments.

As he answered the call, he simply said, "I'm sorry, but your tests show you have invasive breast cancer."

I felt I needed a crash course in breast cancer! I talked with other physicians, nurses, and breast cancer survivors, as well as with my husband, who is educated in health.

Our conference distributed a prayer calendar each year with names of members and leaders to pray for each day. To my great surprise and comfort, our family's name was on the list the very day I learned I had cancer. Thank You, God! Those prayers gave each of us hope and strength to carry us through this process.

As news got out, dear friends and acquaintances shared all kinds of advice and counsel as to what I needed to do to be "cured." One gave me a video by a physician who claimed she was cured by drinking copious amounts of water, avoiding surgery, and living well. Another friend told me I should go to Mexico for special treatments. The recommendations varied widely.

I needed to do some study on my own. By comparing current best scientific practices with what the Bible and Ellen White said about caring for my body temple, we prayerfully decided on a plan. I would include more fruits and vegetables, walk more, drink more water, get more regular sleep, and follow the recommendations of my doctor. Just before my surgery, a small group of close friends came to our house for an anointing service. We sang songs of hope and encouragement, then prayed for God to heal according to His will. But most important, we asked for the strength and courage to be faithful no matter what the outcome.

By His sustaining grace, God has helped me lower my risk factors and become more balanced—more daily walking, drinking more water, including more fruits and vegetables in my diet, getting adequate rest, losing weight, and growing in my trust in my heavenly Father.

By His sustaining grace, God has helped me lower my risk factors and become more balanced.

That was 13 years ago. To this point, I am cancer-free. God has been wonderfully good and faithful to me. He has strengthened my resolve to take care of myself better. As I choose to do what I can, God has done what I could not do! And yet in life, when outcomes may not always be what we hoped for, we can continue to trust our lives to His care, knowing that He works all things together for good to those who love Him.

April Hardinge writes from Silver Spring, Maryland. She loves her family, good music, sewing, gardening, backpacking, and spending time with her wonderful husband. One of her greatest privileges is being the grandmother to four dear grandchildren who love Jesus.